What Our Readers Have Said...

"The Pinpoint Training Series delivers information that could be used in a lot different areas."

•

"Applicable and valid. The information is good."

•

"I like this because I can take them with me to read at a convenient time. I feel the little time I have to spend in the office is best use on activities that directly relate to revenue opportunities. I like the short amount of time it takes to keep up with these."

•

"I just read each book, and then file it for future reference."

•

"My thought is that the real value of these books comes into effect when doing the action plans."

•

"The challenge when I think a specific topic does not apply is to find a way to make it apply."

•

"Easy to use, understand, and reference if needed."

•

"Good layout and to the point."

•

"I think a lot of the recommendations in these books are very useful, and can be applicable to everyday situations. If nothing else, it's a good reference guide to fall back upon if a situation arises in the future."

•

"These books are relevant to today's work environment and the ongoing change in the way we manage our workforce."

•

"These books will pay for the time that I am investing. There are numerous good ideas that will streamline what I do and how I do it."

•

"All and all I think the Pinpoint series is a good program. I know other people I would love to have something like this. I think a lot of the suggestions are very useful, and can be applicable to everyday situations. If nothing else it's a good reference guide to fall back upon if a situation arises in the future."

•

"These books reinforce many concepts that I have learned through seminars, schooling and other programs. For myself, it serves as a constant learning tool that keeps me on top of the issues that many of us encounter every day."

•

"All in all, I think you have good training books. It helps everyone to review these materials, it serves as a good reminder to us on how to conduct ourselves."

•

"The information is valuable in these books."

•

"Good thoughts and ideas."

•

"I believe these books would be valuable to all employees."

•

Strengthening Performance

Pinpoint Management Skill Development Training Series

TIMOTHY F. BEDNARZ

MAJORIUM
BUSINESS PRESS

Pinpoint Management Skill Development Training Series
"Strengthening Performance"
Timothy F. Bednarz

Graphic design: Monika Pawlak

Majorium Business Press
2025 Main Street
Stevens Point, WI 54481
715.342.1018 • 800.654.4935

ISBN 978-1-882181-53-7

Printed in the United States of America

Introduction

The Pinpoint Management Skill Development Training Series is designed for targeted training and education regarding increased improvement in a specific skill or competency.

Each book within this series is designed to be easy to use, understand and apply to your job. It can be used as a basis for training individuals, as a discussion guide or as a personal training tool.

Each chapter within this book discusses a specific concept. When you have completed all eight chapters you should have a 360° perspective of the topic.

Additionally, each chapter is divided into specific sections:

- The first section provides you with an overview of the topic
- The Implications section discusses why the concept is important, and why it is important to learn and apply.
- The Strategies, Tips & Techniques to Apply section teaches how to use and apply the particular concept to your work.
- The Points to Ponder section gives you something to think about or to be discussed with a group setting. These are questions not meant to be immediately answered, but to be pondered over time.
- The Training Activity section provides you with the tools to transfer what you have learned to your job. It is designed to help create an action plan to effectively apply the concept.

Each of the topics in this series is time-tested and proven in the marketplace. They have been used by thousands of employees as training tools. Many of the users have commented that what made these books valuable, was the ability to refer to them when a problem surfaced. They indicated that they remembered reading about the exact problem. They referred back to these books and found an appropriate solution.

You will find them equally valuable as a resource in your professional development library.

Table of Contents

LEARNING OBJECTIVES:

- To identify and apply the elements, factors and principles defining management performance.
- To identify the implications and ramifications of management performance and its impact upon the manager and the organization.
- To overcome problems and pitfalls related to management performance development.
- To apply specific strategies to enhance management performance.
- To analyze the expected results and outcomes of developing and sustaining management performance development, principles and direction.

1

Why Traditional Performance Reviews Are Ineffective

Every organization wishing to monitor ongoing performance must have a method to evaluate both the organization's performance and the individual employee's contribution to it. Evaluating individual performance is a process most managers dread because it represents a source of conflict between the individual manager and the employees he or she directs.

IMPLICATIONS – WHAT THIS MEANS TO YOU

Successful organizations with the capacity to achieve results have managers who are able to communicate productivity expectations to their employees. Managers that include their employees in the decisions on how results will be accomplished create a deeper sense of trust. This trust assures employees the organization is genuinely interested in their needs and communicates that they will be treated with respect. When managers achieve this trust, employees are less likely to believe that the organization will make unfair demands of them.

In addition to trust, employees require accurate performance evaluations assuring that their hard work will be rewarded with tangible benefits. Managers need an effective system to evaluate individual performance in the context of meeting the organization's productivity goals. Traditional performance evaluations are often inadequate and even counterproductive to accomplishing these goals.

STRATEGIES, TIPS & TECHNIQUES TO APPLY

As organizations evolve under the direction of their leaders, the traditional performance evaluation methods they employ have specific deficiencies that actually undermine managers' actions.

The manager defines performance and communicates it through his or her vision. Performance must be evaluated through the individual employee's contribution to the organization. In this regard, traditional performance evaluations are ineffective for the following reasons:

Job Descriptions

Most performance evaluations are based on the individual employee's job description from human resources, and is insufficient in defining the specific functions he or she is expected to perform. In many cases, people with the same job description perform different tasks and have different responsibilities. Additionally, many research studies have demonstrated substantial differences between managers and their people as to what tasks and responsibilities the employee is expected to perform. This discrepancy can be related to the rising expectations of employees as the organization adapts to change, with the principles of leadership being implemented to replace what has been a political bureaucracy in the past.

As these changes have occurred, often in incremental stages, managers have failed to address the rising expectations of their employees to ensure they were in line with the capabilities of the organization.

Employee Ratings

Traditional performance evaluations require managers to rate their employees based upon lists of traits and characteristics that are impossible to measure objectively and accurately.

When employees are rated on a traditional scale it triggers an emotional, often unprofessional reaction. This results in competitive arguments and loss of self-esteem and productivity that undermines any progress a manager may have made.

How employees are rated is also strongly influenced by future administrative actions, such as budget cutbacks or downsizing. In this regard, managers who know that they cannot afford raises or may need to eliminate employees might use these impending actions to justify a lower evaluation. These actions undermine the trust and positive atmosphere that has been built within the organization.

Variations in Evaluative Practices

Differences exist between individual managers. Each has individual biases and personal rating standards, which results in an inconsistency in how employees are evaluated throughout the organization. The same employee can have his performance rated excellent by one manager and fair by another. While the managers who conducted the evaluations may truly believe in their assessments, this disparity increases employee resentment and undermines the entire organization.

The Halo Effect

Studies have shown that managers have a tendency to create a "halo effect" in performance evaluations, where one takes a positive quality they see in another and then extrapolates that positive judgment to all other aspects of that individual. In the case of evaluations, this effect occurs when managers make an initial overall judgment of an employee's performance and then indiscriminately rate all other elements so they are consistent with the overall evaluation. While this often happens unconsciously, it does not produce an accurate and unbiased evaluation of the employee's performance.

Focus on Past Performance Rather Than Future Improvement

Most performance evaluations tend to focus on the employee's past performance including their personal successes and failures without addressing the elements that encourage effective personal performance in the future. While lessons can be derived from past experiences, managers must translate these into actions and activities that the employee can use to enhance their abilities.

Initiation of Conflict

The idea of being evaluated is threatening to the employee and causes problems for both parties involved. People dread being told that they have failed to perform up to acceptable standards or that they have done a poor job. Managers dislike having to be the bearers of bad news and the resulting conflict caused by hurt feelings and lower self-esteem. They know it only undermines what they are attempting to accomplish.

POINTS TO PONDER — SOMETHING TO THINK ABOUT

1. What standards do you use when you evaluate your employees?
2. Do you perceive performance evaluations to be helpful in improving future employee performance?

TRAINING ACTIVITY — APPLICATION & ACTION PLAN

Based upon your personal experiences with past performance reviews:

1. Identify overall and individual problems.
2. Determine the sources of each of the problems you listed.
3. Identify the common reactions to individual performance reviews.
4. Identify the results and consequences you experienced from these reviews.
5. Determine what improvements you would make in the future.

2

Evolving Performance Standards

As an organization evolves in response to the forces of change that it must deal with, managers must also modify their personal methods, including how they view and evaluate their employees' performance. Evaluations must be consistent with the leadership direction and motivational methods employed by other individual managers and should not undermine the progress of the organization.

IMPLICATIONS — WHAT THIS MEANS TO YOU

There is a difference between managers who build an empowered organization, and traditional evaluative methods built around measuring an employee's conformance to specific job expectations. Managing by only seeking to hold employees to job requirements creates internal conflict, dissention and personal rifts, and runs counter to the goals of the manager and the organization.

As organizations evolve, new methods of performance evaluation must be designed and incorporated so that employees feel they are the organization. When this transition is achieved, employees will want to contribute to the organization's success and understand what is needed to accomplish related goals. Therefore, performance evaluation methods must evolve with the organization to involve rather than alienate employees. Evaluations must focus on moving the organization forward through the individual growth and increased competence of its members, rather than on past mistakes and failures. In this manner continued growth is enhanced rather than undermined.

STRATEGIES, TIPS & TECHNIQUES TO APPLY

Traditional performance evaluation methods typically measure the individual employee's performance based upon a rigid set of standards and parameters. Performance is evaluated against a job description rather than by gauging the employee's personal growth and contribution to the achievement of the organization's goals. With this in mind, managers must improve the manner in which they evaluate individual employee performance by using the following guidelines.

Bridge Performance

In an empowered organization, employees cannot simply be evaluated on whether or not they are working according to their job description. As the organization becomes increasingly empowered and evolves in the use of both workgroups and teams, job descriptions become less and less relevant as evaluative tools. Performance increasingly shifts to the group or team and away from the individual as employees work toward mutual goals defined by the shared vision of the manager.

In this light, managers must evaluate the overall performance of the organization they direct and then determine how well the individual employee fits into this larger picture. All performance is intertwined; the individual is ether a strong or weak link in the process. They are evaluated on how well they work within this environment. Managers must use the evaluative process to make the employee's work more meaningful and help them better understand how they fit into the organization and how their job can be more fulfilling.

Evaluate Employee Contributions

Rather than evaluate individual employee's performance against a specific job assignment, managers must evaluate the employee's contributions to the entire organization. In this regard, managers demonstrate to employees that their ideas, insights and personal contributions are both valued and needed if the organization is to succeed.

As organizational empowerment deepens, a synergy develops within each organizational unit, which leads to organizational cohesiveness. Once developed, managers can easily evaluate how well the individual works and operates within this environment and whether they adapt to or fight the transition. It is within this context that managers make this specific evaluation.

Provide Guidance for Growth

Rather than focus on past performance, managers should use the evaluation process to provide their people with the guidance to help them grow and develop their individual capabilities. This support is designed to provide them a path toward increased competence that results in enhanced personal satisfaction. The focus should be on future growth and direction that contributes to overall increased levels of productivity required by the organization. In this context, employees understand what is expected of them as they contribute to the future success of the organization.

Increase Personal Involvement

Within the empowered organization, evaluations are not an "us against them" proposition but a process where employees are involved in the improvement of their own performance. The ratings and conflict associated with traditional performance reviews should be eliminated as employees feel an increase in freedom and self-determination through their involvement in the evaluation.

When the focus of the evaluation shifts to the performance of the organization and the employee's participation toward the accomplishment of mutual goals and objectives, it becomes clear to most employees what they have to do to increase and improve their efforts. This is different than focusing on individual performance and gauging associated faults and problems.

Individuals want to be part of something larger and will work harder to achieve the success of a mutual goal. The synergy and cohesiveness of the organization spurs individual performance on to greater heights. This is clearly demonstrated when sports teams comprised of average players are able to win championships over more talented teams. The mutual goal of the organization likewise brings out the best in everyone when they work together.

POINTS TO PONDER — SOMETHING TO THINK ABOUT

1. Have you adapted your employee performance evaluation style?
2. How can the principles of leadership be incorporated into performance evaluations?

TRAINING ACTIVITY — APPLICATION & ACTION PLAN

Within your own organization, begin to design a personal evaluation system that incorporates the following:

- Bridging performance
- Evaluating employee contributions
- Providing guidance for growth
- Increasing personal involvement

3

Focusing Employees on Common Goals

The overarching principle behind organizational development is that all employees have a wealth of knowledge and experience that can be harnessed and tapped into to enable the organization to grow. Managers are the organization's primary facilitators of knowledge and experience at their specific level. Growth can only be successfully accomplished when employees are focused upon a shared vision and common goals.

IMPLICATIONS – WHAT THIS MEANS TO YOU

With the increasing intensity of global competition, organizations must move forward or be bypassed. With this in mind, organizations wishing to experience growth must ensure that their employees change. Individuals must continue to grow, develop and improve themselves as employees. Organizations are comprised of people; therefore if they are to progress, so must their people.

It is important for managers to understand that they play an important role in the development of the employees they direct. They must create an environment that fosters a learning atmosphere. When they do this, they satisfy the basic human need to continue learning. Most people don't want to stagnate, but seek opportunities to continue their personal development, whether on the job or with hobbies and other areas of interest. Research has shown that most individuals will seek new ways to learn whenever they have the opportunity.

STRATEGIES, TIPS & TECHNIQUES TO APPLY

As managers begin to focus their employees on common goals, there are a number of basic assumptions behind this task. Before managers begin to establish common objectives, they should take the time to review these assumptions with their employees. By doing so, they lay the groundwork of specific expectations that employees can use as a foundation for their goals. These assumptions include:

There Is a Better Way

Many organizations echo the sentiment, "We've been doing it this way for years—why change if it isn't broken?" If this feeling permeates the organization, it signals a level of stagnation in the face of constant change.

There is always a better way of doing things. Research has shown that every time employees review their goals and functions in a group setting they do a superior job of stating them, measuring them and achieving them. This synergy is a clear sign that the organizational unit is growing in terms of its individual members and as a working unit.

Working Capacity

A common complaint is that employees are overworked and have too many demands placed upon them. The truth is that no one is ever working at 100% capacity. Research indicates that even the best performers are only working at a fraction of their true capacity.

There are a number of factors at work here. Some individuals make a conscious choice not to provide the organization with the best of their abilities, for whatever reason. Additionally, many managers are placed in a position where they are applying new leadership principles to old bureaucratic methods with internal resistance present. This resistance often stands in the way of desired levels of effectiveness. In other cases, the speed of change and pace of demands are so overwhelming that managers find it difficult to stop and reorganize effectively.

Motivation

Employees are not strongly motivated to accomplish the goals and objectives established for them by others within the organization. Resistance to authority goes back to childhood, when many resisted their parents and teachers. Most employees feel that the goals established by others underutilize their skills. This resistance is very common in most, if not all, organizations.

However, employees will work hard to achieve goals they set for themselves. They feel empowered and assume ownership of their ideas and concepts. When employees assume ownership, they are motivated to succeed, if only because they have been given an opportunity and do not want to fail. They feel bureaucratic constraints are lifted and they are enthusiastic and challenged by the opportunities presented to them.

Sense of Accomplishment

Employees are happier when they are given the opportunity to accomplish more. Many bridle under older, more bureaucratic rules and procedures that limit their personal ability to perform, grow and develop. Once these constraints are removed, employees have the opportunity to do more than they were allowed in the past. They develop a sense of accomplishment that brings most people pleasure and a feeling of importance.

Most individuals have a need to accomplish something worthwhile in their lives, and managers can use this psychological need to their advantage. If managers are successful in this goal, they will see their employees more interested and enthusiastic than before. The challenge lies in increasing the frequency of these opportunities.

POINTS TO PONDER – SOMETHING TO THINK ABOUT

1. How do the assumptions discussed fit within the current structure and bureaucracy of your organization?
2. Do you believe these assumptions will work to elicit a positive or negative response from your employees? Why?

TRAINING ACTIVITY – APPLICATION & ACTION PLAN

As a basis for helping define the goals and objectives related to increasing employee development, growth and performance, take the time to personally review the assumptions detailed within this lesson, then analyze and discuss them with your people.

1. Talk to your employees about how each assumption alters their perspectives and expectations.
2. Initiate a discussion that elicits feedback that can be used during the development of common goals.

4

Developing Individual Performance Standards

Performance enhancement requires the development of mutually agreed upon goals and measurement standards for use by both managers and employees, which clarifies individual expectations and reduces conflict. It also motivates employees to achieve higher levels of personal performance, as they were responsible for the establishment of these standards, giving them ownership of the ideas and the opportunity to personally grow and develop.

IMPLICATIONS — WHAT THIS MEANS TO YOU

Within the structure of many organizations, managers may need to get upper management approval to implement performance-based standards and evaluations. In some instances, upper management may still require traditional performance rating evaluations. These requirements can pose a challenge to many managers. But managers can introduce performance-based evaluations even when traditional performance rating systems are still used.

It is important for managers to grasp that in certain circumstances they must act on their own initiative to move their organization forward and produce the desired results. They must demonstrate results before management is able to internally change old bureaucratic policies that hinder performance. The ability to lead by results is the essence of leadership.

STRATEGIES, TIPS & TECHNIQUES TO APPLY

The development of individual performance standards doesn't just happen: it must be conceived and nurtured with the cooperative efforts of both managers and employees. Without the mutual agreement of both parties, these standards will be ineffective. With this in mind, managers need to take the following three steps to initiate the implementation of performance standards:

Prepare Employees

If the organization is moving toward empowerment, employees may already be aware of many of the initiatives. However, in other instances managers must take the time to educate individual employees about the changes that are to occur, the reasoning behind them and the expected results.

This preparation cannot be taken lightly if the program is to be successful. Managers may need to introduce the program slowly to surmount resistance, with time provided for employees to express their concerns and offer feedback. If resistance is high, managers may need to influence employees to try the program on an experimental basis.

Gain Mutual Agreement on Job Responsibilities

Managers and employees must reach a mutual agreement on the functions, responsibilities and personal goals of each employee. Most conflict arises when the manager and individual employee have different perceptions and expectations regarding responsibilities.

One especially important area to look at is the employee's job function. Often not described in a job description and going beyond the scope of the individual employee's duties, this area outlines his or her contribution to the organization.

Managers should have each employee prepare a list of his or her job responsibilities, functions and duties. The employee should present their list and mutual agreement should be reached as to the specific meaning of each item. It is essential that both manager and employee clearly understand and agree upon each meaning. While the method of arriving at this agreement will vary from manager to manager, the objective remains the same.

Gain Mutual Agreement on Performance Measurements

Performance measurements inform an employee as to how his or her work is evaluated, not whether it is good or bad. To be effective, the manager and employee must understand the measures that will be used to evaluate the performance of each job function.

Managers should ask individual employees to take their list of job functions, responsibilities and duties and develop a measure for each one of them. As this may be a difficult concept for many employees, the use of the following questions may clarify the issue:

1. How do you know when you're doing a good or bad job?
2. What measurements do you have in mind?
3. What data or facts tell you that you are performing well?

Where possible, employees should be encouraged to develop quantitative measures. However, in some functions, quantitative measures may not be available, so subjective measures may need to be substituted. Some examples of quantitative measures include the number of:

- Rejects
- Errors
- Complaints
- Items produced

In addition to the employee developing his or her own performance standards, managers should create a list of their own. Once done, both lists should be compared, with each standard on both lists individually discussed, compared, modified and mutually agreed upon. Once these standards have been established and agreed upon, both the manager and employee understand how his or her performance will be evaluated, which works to eliminate confusion or conflict at the time of evaluation.

POINTS TO PONDER — SOMETHING TO THINK ABOUT

1. How were your performance standards established in the past?
2. How far do you feel the approach discussed will enhance individual performance within your department, unit or organization?

TRAINING ACTIVITY — APPLICATION & ACTION PLAN

1. Identify various ways performance can be evaluated within your own organizational department or unit. Brainstorming this concept among all employees may be helpful.
2. Once a complete list has been generated, determine the quantitative standards that can be used to measure certain job functions. Identify more subjective standards for others if needed.
3. Use these items when developing performance standards with your individual employees.

5

Establishing Individual Goals and Objectives

The establishment of individual employee goals and objectives can be stressful in many organizations, especially if this is a new concept. Employees often resent being held accountable for their actions. Their perception is that these actions are punitive rather than intended as a mechanism to move the organization forward.

IMPLICATIONS — WHAT THIS MEANS TO YOU

While the establishment of individual goals or objectives is a critical process, managers should recognize that they might be dealing with employee groups with varying degrees of experience in goal setting and implementation.

It is important for managers to understand that these gaps in experience can affect the ultimate success or failure of an individual employee. With this in mind, managers must take steps to help employees succeed, which is dependent upon their personal levels of experience. They must recognize that some employees will need more assistance than others. The key is to dedicate the time required for all to be successful in the attainment of their individual goals.

STRATEGIES, TIPS & TECHNIQUES TO APPLY

The establishment of individual goals and objectives can be a stressful exercise for many employees. Though the process includes elements of an employee review, it is not an evaluation but a process of setting the employee's direction for the future as well as coordinating individual goals with those of the organization. The following techniques and strategies should be utilized to successfully establish individual goals:

Listen

Before a manager begins the formal process of establishing individual goals and objectives with an employee, the first step is to allow the employee the time to express his or her ideas and feelings. This discussion should establish a good mood and should focus on the positive aspects of the employee's job. If complaints are voiced, managers should ask the employee for ways to correct the problem. By giving an employee the opportunity to resolve a problem, the discussion remains focused on the positive aspects of his or her job while empowering them to develop a realistic solution.

Be Forward Looking

Past performance of the employee will undoubtedly become part of the discussion. However, managers should keep the discussion focused on the future goals and objectives and avoid dwelling on past performance issues. This way the employee is focused on his or her future performance and not mired in past problems.

Be Candid

As managers move through the discussion of individual goals and objectives, they must be both candid and honest regarding the employee's abilities so that obtainable goals can be established. This is a constructive, not negative, gesture in that it helps uncover what the employee is capable of and expected to achieve.

Small Steps

To many employees, individual goals can be overwhelming when viewed in their entirety. Managers can effectively ease these fears by breaking long-term objectives down into smaller, short-term targets that move the employee forward. Creating annual, quarterly and monthly goals that both the manager and employee can agree upon is the starting place; it is then the employee's responsibility to break those goals into weekly and daily objectives.

It should be noted that not all employees have the skills to effectively plan their own activities. Managers should review this procedure with their people and perhaps walk them through the process of taking a month's goals and breaking them down into weekly and daily objectives.

Secure Agreement

Once both the employee and manager have developed a realistic set of goals and objectives for the employee and demonstrated how to plan their weekly and daily activities around meeting them, both parties should secure an agreement. The agreement should focus on the individual objectives and how they will be accomplished.

Coordinate

Managers need to have a clear understanding of how each employee plans to reach their goals and the steps that will be taken to accomplish them. However, managers must make sure that all individual goals are aligned with the organization's as well as with those of other unit employees. Failure to do so can result in employees working against each other rather than cooperatively toward the mutual accomplishment of common goals and objectives.

Share

As managers are facilitators, whenever they see an opportunity or need, they should take the time to share their knowledge and expertise with employees regarding how to best reach their individual objectives.

Since goal setting can be a new experience for many employees, they may accept a goal and not know where to start or how to get there. When managers share their expertise, they are facilitating the success of the employee to achieve his or her individual goals. This is what makes the entire process both meaningful and worthwhile.

Remain Task-Oriented

Throughout the process of establishing individual goals and objectives, the climate should be warm, friendly and informal. Yet managers should ensure the process remains task-oriented, as well as be aware that they will need each employee's assistance in the future to help attain their goals. The key is that all should be working together toward the accomplishment of mutual objectives.

Commit to Change

Managers should recognize that the establishment of goals and objectives is a commitment to change. With this in mind, employees may be resistant to change and fear the consequences it may bring. Employees may also be reluctant to commit to goals and objectives out of a personal fear that they will be unable to attain them.

Review

Once the goal setting process has been completed, managers should review each individual objective with the employee. These goals should be committed in writing with both the employee and manager receiving a file copy for future reference.

POINTS TO PONDER — SOMETHING TO THINK ABOUT

1. What goal setting procedures have you used in the past?
2. How do you gauge the degree of employee progress toward goals?

TRAINING ACTIVITY – APPLICATION & ACTION PLAN

Develop a goal setting procedure to be used with your employees. Identify a step-by-step procedure based upon the steps described in this lesson.

- Listen
- Be Forward-Looking
- Be Candid
- Small Steps
- Secure Agreement
- Coordinate
- Share
- Remain Task-Oriented
- Commit to Change
- Review

6

Reading the Pulse of Individual Performance

Managers must employ a series of effective leadership actions in order to adequately assess and analyze employee performance. Individual work must be viewed from varying perspectives and in the context of the entire organization.

IMPLICATIONS — WHAT THIS MEANS TO YOU

Individual employee performance must be linked to the productivity of the organization. Additionally, it must be compared to the levels attained by other employees engaged in similar tasks. Only then can individual performance be evaluated in the proper context—namely, how it fits into overall organizational goals.

Evaluation of individual performance outside of the proper context produces a biased perspective. Linking individual participation to organizational goals and other employee benchmarks allows managers to properly understand and evaluate how an individual is actually performing.

STRATEGIES, TIPS & TECHNIQUES TO APPLY

There are a number of leadership actions that must be utilized when assessing employee performance. An ongoing process, the concept of monitoring the pulse of individual performance demands consistent interaction between managers and the employees under their direction. Managers can facilitate this understanding by engaging in the following behaviors:

Know Your People

Managers should have a knowledge of their employees that goes beyond setting individual performance goals and objectives. Managers must seek daily or regular interaction that allows them to understand their people's work habits, performance abilities and motivations. This contact gives them the ability to conduct a continuous and informal evaluation of their employees' work.

An understanding of their people provides managers numerous benefits. Some employees are more proficient than others in performing specific tasks. Additionally, employees in one job for too long have a tendency to become stale. When managers gain a deeper knowledge of their employees, they are able to use this insight to better match their people to more satisfying tasks or move them into new jobs and areas. The organization is rejuvenated when employees are "rotated" so that they are not performing one job or assignment for too long of a time period.

Insist upon Realism

In most organizational structures there are institutional and personal biases that focus on strengths and minimize weaknesses. This myopic thinking causes individuals to emphasize their positives while ignoring their negatives. This is a natural tendency since no one wants to be thought of poorly or relishes the thought of punitive action.

However, myopic thinking tends to mask the very problems and issues managers must address if the organization is to move forward. Therefore, they must demand realism that presents an accurate picture of individual performance with which to address productivity problems and alter employee behaviors. Change is not undertaken punitively, but in a constructive manner where the employee is assisted in mastering new skills.

Set Clear Goals and Priorities

In the pursuit of increasing organizational performance, the methodology of cooperatively establishing clear goals and priorities cannot be overemphasized.

Goal setting and priorities must be projected beyond individual action so that the sum total of individual goals and priorities attains the overall objectives of the organization. The purpose of individual goal setting is to demonstrate to the employee how they personally fit into the organization's plan and how their performance impacts overall company performance.

Follow Through

Individual plans and goals are of no use if employees are not held to results. Managers must provide their people with information and data that allows them to evaluate their personal performance and hold themselves accountable for the results. Going beyond this, when managers regularly interact with their employees, they are able to monitor their progress and help them achieve their individual goals and objectives. In this capacity managers become both coaches and mentors to their employees, providing insight and advice on how to overcome problems and increase performance.

Reward the Performers

Managers must create an atmosphere where individual performance is recognized. Within union environments, the amount and frequency of certain practical recognition methods, such as pay raises and promotions, may be dictated. However, even within these settings, there are mechanisms available that demonstrate recognition.

Management research dating back to the Westinghouse studies of the 1930s demonstrates the value of recognition in motivating employees and increasing productivity. As recognized in Maslow's Hierarchy of Needs, every human being has a need for personal recognition. However, this recognition is often secondary. The most effective form of acknowledgement is found in the manager publicly expressing appreciation for an employee's work. Other forms of non-monetary recognition may include assigning an employee more challenging tasks.

Expand Employees' Capabilities

As organizations are comprised of people, collective growth and advancement is dependent upon developing their individual capabilities. With this in mind, managers must look for ways to continually push their employees to expand their knowledge, polish their skills and increase their productivity. Beyond the scope of personal motivation, managers must identify opportunities for their employees to enhance their abilities. This process may include one-on-one coaching as well as making specific training and promotional opportunities available to individuals.

Personal motivation includes a manager passionately leading employees by sharing their vision and encouraging group productivity gains. These actions tap into the contagious synergy and energy of an inspired and well-motivated group.

POINTS TO PONDER — SOMETHING TO THINK ABOUT

1. How have you evaluated your employees' behaviors in the past?
2. Do you view individual employee performance in the context of organizational goals and in contrast to other employees' bench-marked performances?

TRAINING ACTIVITY — APPLICATION & ACTION PLAN

While every manager has their own unique leadership style, the following actions should be incorporated into that style.

- Know Your People
- Insist on Realism
- Set Clear Goals and Priorities

- Follow Through
- Reward the Performers
- Expand Employees' Capabilities

1. Decide how well you have already incorporated these behaviors into your style.
2. Identify behaviors that need to be added or improved.
3. Determine methods that will work to incorporate these into your personal style.
4. Make sure to use these new behaviors for a minimum of 30 days in order to make them a habit.

7

Performance Development Increases Effective Decision Making

Decision making can take many forms depending upon the issues being identified and addressed. When managers are making performance-based determinations regarding their organizational units, decisions are typically based on the individual performance of the people under their direction.

IMPLICATIONS — WHAT THIS MEANS TO YOU

Although performance can be documented in tangible and measurable terms, it invariably points to the production or lack thereof of people accountable for specific results. However, decisions regarding these individuals are never made in a void, and hinge on a number of factors.

The development of a performance evaluation program in an empowered organizational environment provides managers the context in which to make more qualified decisions about individual and organizational performance.

STRATEGIES, TIPS & TECHNIQUES TO APPLY

As performance decisions revolve around the individual employees within an organization, the factors outlined below must be considered. Often managers have these factors in the back of their mind, but they should be brought to the forefront when making decisions. It should also be noted that some categories can be objectively measured, while others are intangible and must be viewed in a subjective light. (Where possible, even subjective factors should be linked to something tangible.) In some cases, overall employee performance and behaviors can be benchmarked, affording managers a concrete form of tangible measurement with which to evaluate an employee when decisions need to be made.

Cooperation

Certain employees will cooperate to the extent that they are forced; others will offer efforts beyond what is expected of them. In a union environment, some employees will hide behind negotiated rules to mask their lack of cooperation.

When performance decisions must be made regarding individual employees, their level of cooperation becomes an important consideration. Within the empowered organization, as more decisions are driven down to frontline employees, cooperation becomes an essential factor for the manager.

Enthusiasm

As organizations face continual transformation and evolve into empowerment, individuals may become fearful or resistant to changes. Employees may accept changes because there is no choice, but they will not be enthusiastic. Managers should observe these tendencies because they can produce a drag on the performance of the organization. Additionally, these individuals may influence others and diminish their personal levels of enthusiasm, resulting in further management problems.

Motivation

Personal levels of cooperation and enthusiasm are indicators of the individual employee's motivation. As managers transition their employees into a cohesive organizational unit, employee motivation should shift from a "what's in it for me" focus to a consideration of that which will make the group perform better.

When organizations transition from a more traditional, centralized and polarized bureaucracy to an empowered organization, employees also undergo a transition, although some faster than others. There comes a time when everyone should be motivated by the group rather than the self. An employee's orientation toward self or the organization must be considered in making performance decisions. If one or more employees have a problem in this area, the individual manager must do something to address the situation, or problems can fester and impact the progress of the organization.

Feedback and Insight

Employees in a job for a long period of time develop what is known as "native knowledge." As this knowledge is developed, employees learn much of the specialized information and processes concerning their specific job and responsibilities; they know the shortcuts and techniques they need to take in order to perform more efficiently. Managers must tap into this specialized, highly practical information as well as share it with the rest of their people. However, many longtime employees are reluctant to share their knowledge, as it provides a kind of insurance against lower-paid employees replacing them once they have shared their information.

As managers evaluate their unit's performance, the feedback and insights shared by individual employees must be considered. Through interaction with them, managers should know the level of contribution an employee is capable of providing. They should be aware of those who are sharing their expertise and those who are withholding it, and factor this participation into decisions made regarding performance.

Teamwork

The manager's role is to lead and form their employees into a team focused on mutual goals and objectives. The more cohesive the organizational unit, the more productive and efficient it becomes. Consequently, as decisions are made about performance, the level of teamwork becomes an increasingly important consideration. As decisions are made over time, the degree of teamwork should rise accordingly. If problems are identified with certain individuals, the other factors listed—i.e. cooperation, enthusiasm, motivation and performance—also become issues with these employees. All of these factors are interlinked in the performance evaluation.

Performance

A problem in one or more of the aforementioned factors will contribute to personal performance problems. Conversely, strong positive indications in all of these decision making factors will contribute to enhanced performance.

It should be noted that most evaluations are based upon performance alone. However, when the sum total of these factors are evaluated, the problems behind the lack of performance are highlighted, which makes the manager's decisions more meaningful.

When the root causes behind issues become apparent, it is then easy for decision makers to take the specific actions required to solve the problems.

Uncontrollable Circumstances

The final factor that must be accounted for in a performance evaluation is the impact of uncontrollable events on the organization. There are unquestionably variables—global competition, economic conditions, internal production issues, a West Coast shipping strike—that can significantly impact an individual's work. Whatever the case and circumstances, appropriate allowances must be factored into any performance decision.

POINTS TO PONDER – SOMETHING TO THINK ABOUT

1. When making performance-based decisions, what factors do you traditionally consider?
2. Are there any additional factors directly applying to your employees that could be included?

TRAINING ACTIVITY – APPLICATION & ACTION PLAN

As every organizational environment is different, examine the decision making factors listed below to establish standards and benchmarks for your decision making process. Where possible, create objective, measurable standards on which to base your decisions.

- Cooperation
- Enthusiasm
- Motivation
- Feedback and Insight
- Teamwork
- Performance
- Uncontrollable Circumstances

8

Exploring the Effective Outcomes of Performance

The development of a solid performance management program yields specific overall outcomes that managers need if they are to be successful. In the traditional bureaucratic organization, these programs are often meaningless. However, within the empowered organization an effective performance management program should produce results and move the organization forward in an efficient manner.

IMPLICATIONS — WHAT THIS MEANS TO YOU

As a performance management program is developed and implemented, the role of the manager becomes increasingly important as each one grows in his or her personal abilities as a leader. This means that true leadership capabilities must emerge in crafting clear and understandable goals for his or her people as well as developing simple but effective plans for the organization to follow.

True leadership demands proactive involvement and interaction that removes barriers to performance. As managers mature in their responsibilities, they take their roles more seriously and develop the self-confidence to stretch both themselves and their employees in order to achieve higher levels of productivity and success. They are leaders in the true sense of the word, challenging the old political establishments that stand in the way of performance and overall success.

STRATEGIES, TIPS & TECHNIQUES TO APPLY

The essence of the development of performance standards within the empowered organization is to reach the point where employees direct and evaluate their own performance. The role of the manager is to help them reach mutually agreeable goals and standards and measure progress toward those targets. The manager also provides the guidance, direction and information that the employee needs to evaluate their individual performance against their objectives.

When this level of development is achieved within the organization, several positive outcomes are created that assist both the organization and its managers. These are:

Simplicity

While complexity is the favorite tool of traditional bureaucratic organizations, simplicity is the ally of the manager as leader. The simpler they make their entire organizational structure, the more effective it will become.

As performance standards are established for employees, an understanding should be imparted as to how their work and contributions fit into the organization. Individuals should understand that they are not engaged in mindless tasks, but that their specific efforts add value to the output of the entire organization. When employees see that what they do counts and that there is a clear connection between their job and organizational success, it removes much of the clutter and interference that hampers decision making, which in turn simplifies the process that the organization must undergo to enhance performance and productivity.

Self-Confidence

For the manager, the process allows them to create simple plans with clear targets and objectives. It allows them to communicate more simply with their employees because they understand the connection between their contributions and the organization's success.

When levels of simplicity are achieved within the organization, barriers to progress are removed and cooperation between managers and employees is enhanced. All then understand the results that must be achieved and why they are important. When the entire process is simplified, plans are also more easily implemented and effective, as the hampering complexity traditionally in place within a bureaucratic organization is removed. The more success achieved by managers, employees and the organization, the more self-confidence is established that allows everyone to strive toward more ambitious goals and objectives in the future. Additionally, the performance of all managers and employees is clear to all parties: within a cohesive organizational unit, everyone is accountable to everyone else. This understanding minimizes excuses and wastes less in terms of time as well as financial and operational resources.

Speed

The impact of both simplicity and self-confidence has an overall effect on the speed with which the organization operates. Within the empowered organization, managers and employees have an established and mutually agreeable clear purpose. All parties understand the ramifications of hesitancy in the competitive global marketplace.

The overall goal of performance planning and implementation within the empowered organization is to increase the speed of all internal processes from production, to marketing to overall management. When managers successfully establish clear and understandable goals, simple plans and self-directed evaluation, the barriers to decision making and overall output are effectively removed, enabling the organization to move more nimbly through the forces of change and ongoing competitive pressures.

POINTS TO PONDER — SOMETHING TO THINK ABOUT

1. Do you have a natural tendency to make things simple or more complex than they need to be?
2. What barriers to speed and efficiency do you see within your organization?

TRAINING ACTIVITY – APPLICATION & ACTION PLAN

As simplicity is the ally of the true manager and complexity the favorite tool of traditional bureaucratic organizations, examine your organization and determine how you can simplify the way things are being done. In particular, pay attention to the following elements:

- Goals
- Objectives
- Plans
- Tasks and assignments
- Performance standards and measurements

About the Author

Timothy F. Bednarz, Ph.D. is CEO of the American Management Development Group, Inc. For over 20 years he has researched, designed and authored hundreds of learning and development programs used by Fortune 1000 companies.

He is also the author of *Great! What Makes Leaders Great. What They Did, How They Did It and What You Can Learn from It* (2011).

Speaking Availability

Timothy F. Bednarz, Ph.D. is available for speaking engagements for your next meeting or association event. He can be contacted at 800-654-4935 or by e-mail at timothy.bednarz@majorium.com.

Bulk Sales

Bulk sales of this book or any other titles available from Majorium Business Press. Inquiries can be directed to sales@majorium.com, or by phone at 800-6654-4935.

Quick Order Form

Fax orders: 715-342-1118. Send this form.

Telephone orders: Call 800-654-4935 toll-free. Have your credit card ready.

Email orders: sales@majorium.com

Postal orders: Majorium Business Press, 2025 Main Street, Stevens Point, WI 54481, USA.

Please send the following books:

____

____

____

____

Please send more FREE information on:

❑Catalog ❑Speaking/Seminars ❑Mailing Lists ❑Consulting

Name: ______________________________________

Address: ____________________________________

City: ____________________ State: _____ Zip: __________

Telephone: __________________________________

Email address: _______________________________

Sales tax: Please add 5.5% for products shipped to Wisconsin addresses.

Shipping by air:

United States: $4.00 for first book and $2.00 for each additional product.

International: $9.00 for first book; $5.00 for each additional product (estimate).

Made in the USA
Monee, IL
04 November 2026

67377561R00031